12 GREAT TIPS ON
WRITING TRUE STORIES

by Molly Jones

www.12StoryLibrary.com

12-Story Library is an imprint of Peterson Publishing Company and Press Room Editions.

Produced for 12-Story Library by Red Line Editorial

Photographs ©: Yuri Arcurs/iStockphoto, cover, 1; urbanbuzz/Shutterstock Images, 4; DragonImages/iStockphoto/Thinkstock, 5; Maxiphoto/iStockphoto, 6; Marco Govel/Shutterstock Images, 7; Pamela Moore/iStockphoto, 8; Tatiana Popova/Shutterstock Images, 9; Georgios Kollidas/Shutterstock Images, 10; AVAVA/Shutterstock Images, 12, 29; vitchanan/iStockphoto, 14; Bullstar/Shutterstock Images, 16, 28; olaser/iStockphoto, 17; Suzanne Tucker/Shutterstock Images, 18; Arena Photo UK/Shutterstock Images, 19; A. and I. Kruk/Shutterstock Images, 21; Pixsooz/Shutterstock Images, 22; Iakov Filimonov/Shutterstock Images, 23; Monkey Business Images/Shutterstock Images, 24; skynesher/iStockphoto, 25; dotshock/Shutterstock Images, 26; Dean Mitchell/iStockphoto, 27

Library of Congress Cataloging-in-Publication Data
Names: Jones, Molly, 1933- author.
Title: 12 great tips on writing true stories / by Molly Jones.
Other titles: Twelve great tips on writing true stories
Description: Mankato, MN : 12-Story Library, 2017. | Series: Great tips on
    writing | Includes bibliographical references and index.
Identifiers: LCCN 2016002337 (print) | LCCN 2016003987 (ebook) | ISBN
    9781632352804 (library bound : alk. paper) | ISBN 9781632353306 (pbk. :
    alk. paper) | ISBN 9781621434481 (hosted ebook)
Subjects: LCSH: Biography as a literary form--Juvenile literature. |
    Autobiography--Authorship--Juvenile literature.
Classification: LCC CT22 .J66 2016 (print) | LCC CT22 (ebook) | DDC
    809/.93592--dc23
LC record available at http://lccn.loc.gov/2016002337

Printed in the United States of America
Mankato, MN
May, 2016

Access free, up-to-date content on this topic plus a full digital version of this book. Scan the QR code on page 31 or use your school's login at 12StoryLibrary.com.

Table of Contents

Choose Your Subject

Writing a biography is a big adventure. Biographies tell true stories about real people. Many readers are curious about other people's lives. They want to know how others are like them and how they are different. Sometimes, the subject of a biography has done great things. Readers may want to know how the subject overcame obstacles. Or they want to hear the secret that drove the person to achieve so much. Other times, biographies cover people who have committed crimes or hurt others. Readers want to know what led the subject to act in a certain way.

People read and write biographies because they are curious about others. But biographies also help us understand our own lives. You might find things that you admire about your subject. These things might change the way you think about yourself and your goals. Or maybe you don't want to be like your subject. Writing

Steve Jobs by Walter Isaacson

Biographies are often written about well-known people.

A biography gives a glimpse into someone else's life.

the biography might motivate you to be different.

You might choose to write a true story about yourself. This is called an autobiography. You write down your own memories and feelings. You also write down what others have to say about you. Writing about your own life can help others get to know you better. It can also get you to better know yourself.

No matter who the subject, each biography is a window into someone's life. Whose true story would you like to write?

Quick Tips

- Biographies tell true stories about real people.
- Biographies help readers learn about themselves.
- In an autobiography, the writer is the subject.

TRY IT OUT

Make a list of people you would like to write about. Whom are you most curious about? Maybe you want to know more about a famous person or a distant relative. Or maybe you want to know more about your own childhood.

Map the Scope of Your Story

Every true story is unique because every person is unique. There are billions of possible stories you can tell. But choose your subject carefully. You will be spending a lot of time learning about your subject's life.

Once you've picked someone to write about, you now need to think about what part of the person's life you want to cover. No biographer can tell everything about someone's life. There is

not enough time or information to do so. All biographers must choose what to include and what to leave out. Many biographies start with a person's birth and end with the person's death. Others focus on a smaller time frame or aspect of the person's life. For example, imagine you want to tell the story of how an Olympic sprinter won her first gold medal. You would want to focus on her history as a runner. The person might also be a great singer. But you would probably focus on her first

There are many potential subjects to choose from.

track-and-field meet instead of her first choir concert.

Your task as biographer is to recreate the subject in words. The aim is to make your subject interest your readers as much as he or she interests you. To do this, find out what interests you the most about your subject. Read about the person. Take notes. Begin to sketch an outline of the person's life. What area are you most interested in? It might be a short time frame that sticks out to you. Or maybe it's one relationship or area of interest that stretches throughout the person's life.

Quick Tips

- Biographies cannot cover everything about a person's life.
- Some biographies start with the person's birth and end at the person's death.
- Some biographies focus on a specific time frame or theme.
- Choose the time frame that will be most interesting to you and your readers.

TRY IT OUT

Consider writing about yourself. Describe at least three characteristics you think readers would be interested in knowing more about.

Mine for Gold in Your Research

There are many ways to learn the details of your subject's life. Primary sources are best. These are sources that give firsthand accounts of your subject's life. For example, they might be your subject's diaries or letters. Primary sources might also be written by people who saw your subject do something. For example, maybe someone wrote about the event in the newspaper. Take notes on your primary sources. Make sure you put in your notes where each bit of information came from. Doing so will help you later on.

Primary sources are those who witnessed events firsthand.

Quick Tips

- Primary sources provide the best information.
- These sources can be books, articles, or people.
- Include the name of the source in your notes.
- Interviews can help you fill gaps in your research.

People can also be primary sources. You can get information from these people through interviews. If your subject is alive, you can talk to him or her. But it is also good to hear from others. Neighbors, friends, teachers, family members, and colleagues can all help you better know your subject. They may be able to tell you new and interesting facts and stories. They can also answer

An audio recorder can help refresh your memory of an interview.

any questions you have not been able to answer with your research.

Before an interview, think about questions you want to ask the person. Be prepared to make notes about their responses. You can also use an audio recorder to record the conversation. This way, you can listen back later for anything you were unclear about in your notes. If the person's answers make you think of new things, ask follow-up questions to learn more. One great part of interviewing is that it can be surprising. Talking to others can help you explore areas you may not have thought about.

TRY IT OUT

Pick a person to interview who knows your subject well. Make a list of five questions you'd like to ask that person about your subject.

9

Give Important Background Information

Many influences combine to make your subject's story. Some of these influences are general, such as the era in which the person lived or the country in which he or she was born. Other influences are more specific, such as the quality of the school in the person's town. Some influences are very specific, such as the person's relationship with his or her family.

Think of your writing as a portrait of your subject. These influences make up the background for the portrait. They give your story context. Giving your readers context helps them understand your subject better. Imagine you

If your subject is a man from 17th-century Europe, it may be important to say that men at that time wore wigs.

CONTEXT

Background information helps readers get to know your subject. Notice the difference between the following examples:

Little context:

> When he was 16, he was brought from Africa to North America. There, he worked digging farm roads across the plantation of a rich landowner.

More context:

> He stood on the dock outside the ship. His father's words, spoken half a world away, were recorded in his diary: *Never allow them to make you less than a man.*

> "Take him that way," the slave owner said. "Chain him. Give him a pick."

are writing about a man from the 1600s. You learn that he wore a long white wig. If you do not tell readers that wigs were common for men at that time, they might get the wrong impression about your subject. You want your portrait to be as accurate as possible.

Think about what your readers will need to know about your subject's background. Research the town the person grew up in. Read newspapers from that time period. Doing these things will help you understand your subject better. As you write, make sure the subject's background is clear to your readers.

Quick Tips

- Many things make your subject's story unique.
- Context helps readers understand your subject.
- Context can be general or specific.

Consider Your Audience

Whom are you writing for? Some readers may know more about your subject than others. For example, your teacher may know more about your subject than your classmates. So, writing for your teacher would be different from writing for your peers. Thinking about your readers will help you decide what information to include in your stories. It will also help you know how to present it.

Think about who will be reading your story.

Imagine you are writing a biography about a famous scientist. If you are writing for your science teacher, you may not need to spend as much time giving background information. Your teacher will probably know some things about the person. You can focus on the person's career and work. But maybe you are writing to tell your classmates about the person. In this case, you might need to spend more time on your subject's background. You might try to cover the most important events in the subject's career.

Thinking of your reader also affects what words you use. You might have learned complicated words when researching your subject. Using these words might confuse some readers. You may need to explain them in detail. Or you might just use easier words that help your readers understand what you are saying.

AUDIENCE

If your readers know a lot about a subject, you can use more advanced words:

> He was a state legislator. He is now retired and receives Social Security.

If your readers know less about a topic, you may need to explain more:

> He was a member of the state legislature, the group of people that makes state laws. Now, he no longer works. He gets money each month from Social Security, a government program that helps older people pay their bills.

Quick Tips

- Think about who will likely read your work.
- Give enough background information for your readers.
- Use words your readers will understand.

13

6

Grab and Hold Your Reader's Attention

You want readers to pay attention to what you have to say. To make sure they do, grab their attention from the first sentence. Make them want to learn more. One way to do this is to start your story with an exciting or unusual event. Everything in your biography must be true. But that does not

mean your story needs to be boring. You can use storytelling techniques to keep your readers interested.

One way to grab your audience's attention is to create suspense. For example, imagine you are writing about a racecar driver. You might start your story with a car crash the driver was

Using storytelling techniques can help engage readers.

in as a teen. The reader will want to know what happened next that made the driver a racing champion.

You can also surprise your audience in your opening. For example, you might start a book about a famous actress by talking about her dog. This type of opening will surprise the readers. It will make them wonder what her dog has to do with acting. You could then say that she practiced all of her movie lines in front of her dog.

Continue to keep your readers wondering what will happen next. Doing so will make your writing more engaging and memorable.

Quick Tips

- Grab your audience's attention from the start.
- Include suspense or a surprise in your opening.
- Make sure the events in your story are true.

OPENING STRONG

Does the following opening make you want to read more? Why or why not?

She lay still in the hospital bed. The only thing moving was the machine next to her, helping her breathe. Her eyes were open. She was deep in thought. Would she ever move again? Would she ever breathe again by herself?

What about this opening?

He sat up in his seat. His fingers were gripped together to keep them still. Slowly a woman walked onto the stage to present the journalism award. He had borrowed an audio recorder for interviews. He had written through many nights. Finally, just hours before the deadline, he had turned in his article. But did others believe his work was worth an award?

7

Stick with the Facts

All writers want readers to be excited about their stories. But when writing a biography, the most important thing is to tell the truth. When people read true stories, they expect that everything in the stories actually happened. This makes research a very important part of your work. Details that you cannot find in your research must be left out, not created. If you make up any part of your story, you cannot call it true. Otherwise, you mislead your readers. There are a number of things to keep in mind that will help your story stay truthful.

First, use only quotations that you know were actually spoken. Do not

All details in a biography must come from a source.

Details such as the weather help set the scene for your story.

make up any part of a conversation. Using primary sources will help you make sure your quotes are accurate.

Second, do not make up emotions for people. Imagine you are interviewing your subject and think he looks unhappy. You cannot say he feels angry unless he says that he does. It might seem obvious to you that he is upset. But you need evidence to support your writing. Instead of saying he is angry, you can describe how he looks. Maybe you see him scowl. You can say that instead. This is more truthful. It is also more interesting. It helps the reader imagine what the man looks like.

Visual details help make readers more interested in your writing. But keep in mind, if you say, "It was a windy, rainy night," you need evidence that this was true.

Quick Tips

- All of your details must be true.
- Quote words you know were actually spoken.
- Do not assume you know your subject's emotions.

Write with Style

As you write your true story, think about what images your words create for your readers. One way to make your images more exciting is to write in active voice. In active voice, the subject of the sentence does the action. "Jaylen hit the ball," is an example of active voice. In passive voice, the subject receives the action:

"The ball was hit by Jaylen." Active voice helps readers imagine the action happening as they read. Words like *run*, *fly*, *persuade*, *hit*, *conquer*, and *explode* create clear images for readers. On the other hand, words like *be*, *was*, *is*, and *has* fail to create a sense of action. Use

Active verbs, such as *swing* and *hit*, give a sense of action to your writing.

active words when you write about your subject's life.

Choosing precise words also helps hold your reader's attention. Use your thesaurus to find words that express your exact meaning. For example you might say, "Sam was excited." But using a more specific word helps the reader understand what you mean. Do you mean frantic, agitated, angry, or ecstatic?

> Thesauruses can help you find the exact word you want.

Quick Tips

- Write in active voice.
- Use words that give your story action and emotion.
- Use words that say exactly what you mean.

ACTIVE AND PRECISE

Maybe your subject is an award-winning ecologist. You could write, "He was always interested in plants and animals. But he had never played sports." Or you could make your writing more active and precise: "Every evening, while his friends were at baseball practice, he sat under an old sassafras tree. He sketched the beetles, spiders, and grasshoppers he saw. They crawled and jumped around him."

Use Connections and Transitions

As you tell your true story, you will cover many different things. You might jump from when your subject was 11 years old to when he or she was 25. Or you might go from writing about the subject's family to writing about his or her work. If you jump from one idea to another too quickly, your readers may lose interest. How can you make your writing hard to put down? Connections and transitions can help.

TRY IT OUT

Use transitions to make the following paragraph clearer:

My sister learned to cook on a woodstove. Our mother always cooked on a woodstove. My sister, who travels a lot, bought an electric stove.

FITTING TOGETHER

Leaving out transition words can make sentences confusing:

Graduate students at big universities hold tutoring sessions for math and science classes. Francis is happy he went to a small college. Individual students receive more attention.

By adding a few transitional words, the sentences seem logical:

At big universities, graduate students hold tutoring sessions for math and science classes. However, Francis still believes small colleges are best because individual students receive more attention.

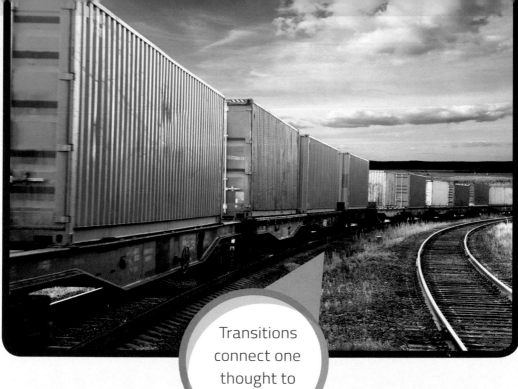

Transitions connect one thought to another.

Connections help readers understand how ideas and actions fit together. For example, your story might feel like it is saying, "this happened, this happened, and this happened." But with connections, you can make it sound like "this happened, causing this to happen, which made this happen." Connections help readers see how events are related. Connections help your story flow smoothly from one event to the next.

Similarly, good transitions tie one sentence to another. Words and phrases such as *in addition*, *similarly*, *since*, *also*, and *because* help readers see how one sentence relates to the next.

Quick Tips

- Connections and transitions help your readers follow your thoughts.
- Use connections to show how one event relates to another in your story.
- Use transition words to show how sentences relate to each other.

Apply the Four Steps for Successful Revision

Once you've written your true story, it is time to revise. All good writers revise their work. It is a part of the writing process. Before you consider your true story complete, take these four steps. They will help make your work the best it can be.

Step 1: Proofread your manuscript. Look for phrases that are not complete sentences and for grammar errors. Look for misspelled words and punctuation mistakes. A spell-checker can help. But make sure not to rely on it too much to find errors.

Step 2: Reread your story. Look for completeness and smoothness. Be sure you haven't left out information

All writers need to read and revise their work.

Having a friend read your work can help you learn about your writing.

you meant to include. Also, be sure your information is organized in a way that makes sense.

Step 3: Read your work aloud. Often, hearing your words spoken points out rough wording. It also makes it easier to hear bad transitions.

Step 4: Trade stories with another writer. Talk about ways each of your pieces can be improved.

Quick Tips

- Proofread your work to fix spelling and grammar errors.
- Reread your work to make sure you have included all your information.
- Read the story aloud to listen for smoothness and completeness.
- Share your work with another writer and listen to his or her comments.

11

Give Credit to Your Sources

You have finalized the information you want to include in your biography. Now, it is time to give credit to the sources you used. Maybe you used quotations from another book about your subject. Or maybe you used data from an interview with someone familiar with the person. These sources have helped you write your biography.

You must give them credit for their work. Your readers will appreciate you including your sources. Showing where you got information helps readers feel confident you are telling the truth. It also shows them where they can find more information, if they are curious.

Online sources also need to be given credit.

Quick Tips

- Including your sources gives credit to those whose information you have used.
- Including your sources helps readers feel confident in your work.
- Giving credit to your sources starts during research.

Giving credit to your sources is one of the last things you do when writing your true story. But the process begins with your research. As you read primary sources and conduct interviews, it is important to keep track in your notes of where each piece of information comes from. Do not expect to remember later where the information came from. You do not want to have to go back through your sources looking for the information you used.

> Using others' work to help you write is not bad, but you must give them credit.

There are many ways to give credit to your sources. Sometimes, sources are placed at the bottom of the page on which the borrowed information appears. Other times, sources are added at the end of your writing. If you are writing your biography for class, ask your teacher how he or she would like you to credit your sources.

25

Share Your Polished Work with Others

Your biography tells an important story. Now it is time to share your discoveries with others. There are many ways you can share your work. Your school or community might have a group for young writers. These groups are great ways to get feedback on your work. Writing groups also give you the opportunity to see how others write. If your school or community doesn't have a writing group, talk to an adult about starting one. Or start one with your friends or classmates.

There are also many groups that publish student writing

A writing group works to polish each others' work.

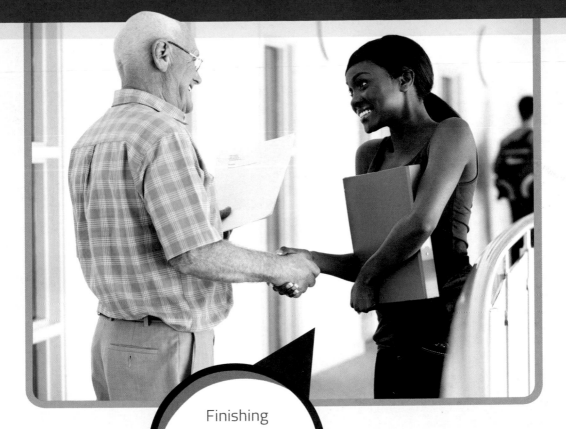

of all kinds. Have an adult help you find magazines, colleges, or websites that publish the work of students. Read the guidelines, rules, and instructions before sending your work. If your work is not selected, read those that are published. Learn what they do well and try again.

Finishing a writing project is a big accomplishment.

have written. Learn from any feedback you get. Then get busy writing something new!

You can use a printer to make hard copies of your work. Whether many people read your work or only your teacher does, be proud of what you

Quick Tips

- Look for a writing group where you can share your work.
- Submit your work for publication.
- Print your work to share and save.
- Be proud of your accomplishment.

Writer's Checklist

✓ Choose a subject you would like to know more about.

✓ Decide on the scope of your story.

✓ Research using primary sources.

✓ Imagine your typical reader, and write for that person.

✓ Grab your reader with an exciting opening.

✓ Give your readers background information.

✓ Do not make anything up.

✓ Use good transitions and good connections.

✓ Write with active and precise words.

✓ Proofread for completeness and smoothness.

✓ Have others read your work.

✓ Give credit for the research of others.

✓ Share your work with others.

Glossary

autobiography
A true story written by a writer about herself or himself.

biography
A true story about the life of a real person, either living or no longer living.

connections
Words or phrases that show how one idea or event is related to another.

context
The conditions surrounding a situation.

ecologist
Someone who studies the relationships between organisms and their environments.

interview
A meeting in which someone asks someone else questions.

mislead
To cause someone to believe something that is not true.

peer
A person of the same age group or social group as someone else.

spell-checker
A computer program that finds and corrects writing errors.

subject
The person or thing discussed.

suspense
When the reader doesn't know what is going to happen.

time frame
A period of time used for a particular project.

transitions
Words or phrases that tie one sentence or paragraph to another.

For More Information

Books

Fogarty, Mignon. *Grammar Girl Presents the Ultimate Writing Guide for Students*. New York: Henry Holt, 2011.

Lee, Hermione. *Biography: A Very Short Introduction*. Oxford, UK: Oxford University Press, 2009.

Peterson, Brenda, and Sarah Jane Freymann. *Your Life Is a Book: How to Craft and Publish Your Memoir*. Seattle, WA: Sasquatch Books, 2014.

Schwartz, Tina P. *Writing and Publishing: The Ultimate Teen Guide*. Lanham, MD: Scarecrow Press, 2010.

Visit 12StoryLibrary.com

Scan the code or use your school's login at **12StoryLibrary.com** for recent updates about this topic and a full digital version of this book. Enjoy free access to:

- Digital ebook
- Breaking news updates
- Live content feeds
- Videos, interactive maps, and graphics
- Additional web resources

Note to educators: Visit 12StoryLibrary.com/register to sign up for free premium website access. Enjoy live content plus a full digital version of every 12-Story Library book you own for every student at your school.

Index

About the Author

Molly Jones, Ph.D., is author of 13 fiction and nonfiction books and a number of magazine articles for young readers. She lives on Lake Murray, in the midlands of South Carolina.